Shivoham

KEEP THE EARTH ALIVE – HOW TO LIVE

KOTA. RAMALINGAIAH

Table of Contents

Shivoham*

Keep the Earth ALIVE - How to LIVE on Earth* Everyone must Remember the NAME of God anywhere*

The Happiness & Pain of all worldly creatures are the same*

Now United Nation responsibility for save the Earth & Earthly Creature!

If any problem happens with the Alliance! It should be addressed to all the countries and have to be solved together.

If there is a problem between the two countries, the U.N should inform all nations about the issue and solve them.

Whose Nation their Home. It's good - But we living on this Earth - It's should know. As we think! That's all - That is Country, Foreign or any Planets - Alliance! Earth belongs to Living things - Not only Human*

This earth is about 8400,000 inhabitants. It is not advisable to harm for Animals, Birds, Living things, Environment & You. Everything is worth it. The HARMFUL Experiments that you have taken on Country or land - Do not seem to be good for Living things & Earth. This is our Home because we all living on the Earth. Now we are all Earthly Creature*

I have come to spread the Devotion & the Virtue on-line in all the Earthly Creatures. This is God's will. So please everyone can cooperate.

It's our border don't cross

Everyone must remember the Name of GOD Everywhere.

The Happiness & Pain of all Lordly creatures are the SAME.

© Jose B. Ruiz/naturepl.com

Now United Nation responsibility for save the Earth & Earthly Creature!

**Earth is not your's -
Don't use harmfully
experiment.**

Shiva*

Must save & live simply - safely.

This is LIFE

Must remember the Name of GOD

NASA

JUST LIVE WITH TOGETHERNESS

DON'T CROSS LIMITS.

SHIVOHAM

TOTAL LIFE ONLY FOR EARTHENWARE.

Agriculturist

SAVE TREES
SAVE FORESTS
SAVE WILDLIFE
SAVE EARTH
SHIVOHAM

PROTECT & SAVE

13

17

KEEP THE EARTH ALIVE – HOW TO LIVE

KOTA. RAMALINGAIAH